BASIC
CHRISTIANITY

21 DAY GUIDE TO FOLLOWING JESUS

Basic Christianity
English
Copyright 2016
ISBN 978-0-692-77544-8
Edition 1, Printing 1
500 copies

Visit our website: Basics-NYC.com

PARKER + JESSI GREEN

WHERE NOW THAT EVERYTHING HAS CHANGED

JESUS CHRIST DIED AND ROSE AGAIN SO THAT
WE MAY HAVE LIFE AND HAVE IT TO THE FULL.

WELCOME

Welcome to the family! We are so glad you have made the decision to begin following Jesus. This 21 day journey will help you along The Way. One very important thing we need to highlight before you get started.

The best and most effective way to go on this journey is with other followers of Jesus. We suggest that you ask your pastor or leader who they could connect you with to get started.

We are praying for you and want you to know that God loves you more than you'll ever be able to discover in this lifetime.

Our prayer for you on this eternal adventure:

"THE LORD BLESS YOU AND KEEP YOU;

**THE LORD MAKE HIS FACE SHINE ON YOU
AND BE GRACIOUS TO YOU;**

**THE LORD TURN HIS FACE TOWARD YOU
AND GIVE YOU PEACE."**

NUMBERS 6:24-26

DAY 01

ROMANS 8:1

Ask God to forgive you for your sins and write down below what He has forgiven you from:

_____

_____

_____

_____

_____

_____

_____

_____

_____

_____

_____

_____

_____

_____

_____

DAY 02

1 Set aside time daily

2 Worship Jesus - you can do so by playing music or just talking about how great God is

3 Thank God for all that He has done

4 Using scripture as a guide (The Psalms) begin to say out loud what comes to your mind and heart to God

5 Allow moments of silence and write down what you hear. If what you hear in your heart doesn't contradict the word of God (the bible) and it glorifies Jesus. God the Holy Spirit is having a conversation with you

6 Ask Jesus to save those you love

7 Ask Jesus to provide for all your needs

A BRAND NEW LIFE

DAY 03

Baptism is a public declaration that you have been raised from death to life and are now a follower of Jesus. When baptized, you are submerged under the water (representing death) then rise up again (representing life). Jesus commands us to do this as His followers.

Today, talk to someone in your church, or a Jesus follower you know, about getting baptized.

Add a picture of your baptism here and any special memories from the day

DAY 04

These two spiritual disciplines often go hand in hand as you develop your relationship with Jesus. We suggest that you wake up 30 minutes earlier than usual and go to a quiet place.

Direct your heart and mind by using Scripture, especially the books of Matthew, Mark, Luke, or John. Keep a pen and notepad nearby for when you're distracted by things to do; simply write them down quickly on the pad and refocus.

Continue to do this over the next 21 days - every day.

DAY 05

PRAY WITH THESE VERSES

HEAL

"HE HEALS THE BROKENHEARTED AND BINDS UP THEIR WOUNDS."

PSALM 157:3

MY

"MY FLESH AND MY HEART MAY FAIL, BUT GOD IS THE STRENGTH OF MY HEART AND MY PORTION FOREVER."

PSALM 73:26

HEART

"BUT HE SAID TO ME, 'MY GRACE IS SUFFICIENT FOR YOU, FOR MY POWER IS MADE PERFECT IN WEAKNESS.'"

2 CORINTHIANS 12:9

NOTES

DAY 06

Hearing God may seem impossible, however God wants you to hear Him even more than you want to hear Him. You were created to hear God's voice! He loves you and wants a relationship with you. Hearing the voice of God will transform your life. Here are a couple of ways to "tune in" to hearing God's voice when you get started on this journey.

- Find a quiet place alone and remove all distractions. Devote yourself to time with Jesus – make it special and intentional.
  (Remember the solitude and silence from day 4)

- Read the Bible daily at a specific time and place. Reading the Bible will help you learn how God speaks.

- Write down thoughts, words, and/or feelings you have during prayer.

_____

_____

_____

_____

_____

_____

_____

_____

_____

_____

_____

_____

_____

NOTES

DAY 07

A church is not a building. The church is a group of people that are following Jesus together. You're not meant to do life alone.

Find a church that makes disciples of Jesus. Right away, become a participant – not just a spectator. Being a "consumer christian" will leave you feeling like something is missing, and it will indeed be missing.

The best thing you can do is serve the 'body' of Christ as soon as possible. Write down the church you will join and the next steps you'll take to invest into that community.

"THIS IS HOW WE KNOW WHAT LOVE IS: JESUS CHRIST LAID DOWN HIS LIFE FOR US. AND WE OUGHT TO LAY DOWN OUR LIVES FOR OUR BROTHERS AND SISTERS."

1 JOHN 3:16

WHY OTHER PEOPLE MATTER

DAY 08

JESUS

"1 In the beginning was the Word, and the Word was with God, and the Word was God. 2 He was in the beginning with God. 3 All things were made through him, and without him was not any thing made that was made. 4 In him was life, [a] and the life was the light of men. 5 The light shines in the darkness, and the darkness has not overcome it."

JOHN 1:1-5

Jesus is a real person. He is fully alive and active in your life. He knows you, and you can know Him. Jesus isn't just a historical character. The things written in the gospels are things He actually did. He sweat, He bled, He slept outside, He got angry, calmed storms, helped and healed the sick and hungry, He ate dinner with friends, He laughed, He wept. He is the center, purpose, and Savior of all we do. He is the King of all things created, your closest friend, and your sacrifice. He loves you. When life is good and when life is terrible, think on Jesus: who He is and what He has done and is still doing for you.

Try today, throughout every activity to stop for a moment and think about Jesus. Use scripture (maybe on a note card or on your device) to help your mind learn about Him and focus on Him.

Remember, Jesus is present with you by the Holy Spirit. He's not a far off person you're just dreaming about.

DAY 09

The Bible says "The Word became flesh." Jesus is the Word. When you read the Bible it isn't just words - it is a way to pursue your relationship with Jesus. The Word will come alive in your daily life and change you from the inside out.

Read it, think on it, say it out loud, pray it, sing it, meditate on it, DO what it says. Interacting daily with the Word of God will make you come alive.

"For the Word of God is alive and active. Sharper than any double-edged sword, it penetrates even to dividing soul and spirit, joints and marrow; it judges the thoughts and attitudes of the heart."
HEBREWS 4:12

Write down a verse in the Bible that you want to memorize.

_____

_____

_____

_____

_____

_____

_____

_____

_____

_____

_____

DAY 10

PRAY WITH THESE VERSES

SPEAK

"TRUST IN THE LORD WITH ALL YOUR HEART, AND LEAN NOT ON YOUR OWN UNDERSTANDING; IN ALL YOUR WAYS ACKNOWLEDGE HIM, AND HE SHALL DIRECT YOUR PATHS."

PROVERBS 3:5-6

TO

"YOUR EARS SHALL HEAR A WORD BEHIND YOU, SAYING, 'THIS IS THE WAY, WALK IN IT,' WHENEVER YOU TURN TO THE RIGHT HAND OR WHENEVER YOU TURN TO THE LEFT."

ISAIAH 30:21

ME

"THEN YOU WILL CALL UPON ME AND GO AND PRAY TO ME, AND I WILL LISTEN TO YOU. AND YOU WILL SEEK ME AND FIND ME, WHEN YOU SEARCH FOR ME WITH ALL YOUR HEART."

JEREMIAH 29:12-13

NOTES

DAY 11

GOD THE FATHER

"I give them eternal life, and they shall never perish; no one will snatch them out of my hand. My Father, who has given them to me, is greater than all ; no one can snatch them out of my Father's hand. I and the Father are one."

JOHN 10:28-30

God the Father is the originator and the author of all things. Jesus and the Father are one, along with the Holy Spirit. They are a perfect community together. Jesus said while He was on earth that He would only do what He saw the Father doing.

God the Father is absolute in His power and majesty and the ruler of the universe. Our Father also provides for every detail of our life, loves us beyond what we can comprehend, and sent us His son to die for our sins and receive the wrath we deserved. He is a perfect Father.

Pray that our good and perfect Father's will would be done in your life.

DAY 12

THE HOLY SPIRIT

"But very truly I tell you, it is for you good that I am going away. Unless I go away, the advocate will not come to you; but if I go, I will send Him to you."

JOHN 16:7

The Holy Spirit is a person and the Advocate; a person that is living and active all around us, and even lives inside of us. When Jesus went to heaven, He promised that the Holy Spirit would come and that we would be clothed with power from on high. We are given the ability to carry out the will of God by the Holy Spirit living in us, and transforming us daily to be like Jesus. The Holy Spirit is God, and not a power to be wielded. The Holy Spirit reveals the meaning of scripture to us, and gives us power to do what it says.

Ask the Holy Spirit to reveal Himself to you, and pray for more of the Holy Spirit like Jesus talks about in Luke 11:13.

"So if you sinful people know how to give good gifts to your children, how much more will your heavenly Father give the Holy Spirit to those who ask him."

LUKE 11:13

DAY 13

PRAY WITH THESE VERSES

FILL ME

"AND THEY WERE ALL FILLED WITH THE HOLY
SPIRIT AND BEGAN TO SPEAK IN OTHER TONGUES
AS THE SPIRIT GAVE THEM UTTERANCE."

ACTS 2:4

WITH YOUR

"AND WHEN THEY HAD PRAYED, THE PLACE IN
WHICH THEY WERE GATHERED TOGETHER WAS
SHAKEN, AND THEY WERE ALL FILLED WITH THE
HOLY SPIRIT AND CONTINUED TO SPEAK THE
WORD OF GOD WITH BOLDNESS."

ACTS 4:31

SPIRIT

"AND THE DISCIPLES WERE FILLED WITH
JOY AND WITH THE HOLY SPIRIT."

ACTS 13:52

NOTES

DAY 14

Now that Jesus has forgiven you, nobody owes you anything. This can be a hard truth to swallow, but, try and focus here on how much Jesus loves you and all He did for you.

Make a list of people you need to forgive and say out loud that you forgive them and you release them of anything they owe you. This can be difficult. You may want to have someone you trust that's following Jesus do this with you. Jesus wants you to be completely free to love yourself and others. This is a crucial key to your freedom.

Go for it!

DAY 15

JESUS IS ALIVE

If He is dead, then the whole premise of Christianity goes out the window. The fact that Jesus is alive is a life transforming fact. Jesus is not an idea, or a principle - He is a living breathing person that cares about your daily life.

When Jesus rose from the dead, it meant that we no longer need to fear anything. Think about what's possible with Jesus!

"Jesus said to her, 'I am the resurrection and the life. Whoever believes in me, though he die, yet shall he live, and everyone who lives and believes in me shall never die. Do you believe this?'"

JOHN 11:25-26

Read this verse and ask God what this means for you.

NOTES

DAY 16

Fasting is depriving yourself of a meal or meals over a period of time to find your nourishment in Jesus. Choose a meal to give up to start, and move towards a day or days over time. This spiritual discipline will give you clearer communication with God and help you focus on what really matters. At times, it will expose the areas that you need the grace (power) of Jesus to reach in and transform you. Take the time that you would normally spend eating, and dwell on Jesus instead.

Use scripture to help focus your heart and mind with a written note card, device, or your Bible.

"Jesus answered, 'It is written: 'Man shall not live on bread alone, but on every word that comes from the mouth of God.'"

MATTHEW 4:4

DAY 17

PRAY WITH THESE VERSES

HEAL

"DO NOT BE CONFORMED TO THIS WORLD, BUT BE TRANSFORMED BY THE RENEWAL OF YOUR MIND, THAT BY TESTING YOU MAY DISCERN WHAT IS THE WILL OF GOD, WHAT IS GOOD AND ACCEPTABLE AND PERFECT."

ROMANS 12:2

MY

"FOR GOD GAVE US A SPIRIT NOT OF FEAR BUT OF POWER AND LOVE AND SELF-CONTROL."

2 TIMOTHY 1:7

MIND

"FINALLY, BROTHERS, WHATEVER IS TRUE, WHATEVER IS HONORABLE, WHATEVER IS JUST, WHATEVER IS PURE, WHATEVER IS LOVELY, WHATEVER IS COMMENDABLE, IF THERE IS ANY EXCELLENCE, IF THERE IS ANYTHING WORTHY OF PRAISE, THINK ABOUT THESE THINGS."

PHILIPPIANS 4:8

NOTES

DAY 18

Who you are is no longer defined by what you do or where you've been.

It's all defined by Jesus and HIS work. So who are you?

Everything flows from this new relationship. When Jesus says we must be 'born again' - we are born into a new family. Think about how a loving God treats his kids. You have everything you need already in Him.

"See what great love the Father has lavished on us, that we should be called children of God! And that is what we are!"
1 JOHN 3:1

Ask God who he says you are and write it down here:

_____

_____

_____

_____

_____

_____

_____

_____

_____

_____

_____

_____

_____

_____

NOTES

DAY 19

Worship isn't just singing in church. Worship is what we do with our lives. Every single thing we do, can and should glorify God.

"Therefore let us be grateful for receiving a kingdom that cannot be shaken, and thus let us offer to God acceptable worship, with reverence and awe."

HEBREWS 2:28

What part(s) of your life can you start to intentionally give to Jesus?

DAY 20

Financial giving can be divided into two categories: tithes and offerings. The Bible teaches us that we worship the Lord with our tithe, which is ten percent of our income contributed to the church on a regular basis. When we feel called to give over and above our tithe, we do so as an offering.

"They had everything in common 32 now the full number of those who believed were of one heart and soul, and no one said that any of the things that belonged to Him was His own, but they had everything in common. 33 and with great power the apostles were giving their testimony to the resurrection of the Lord Jesus, and great grace was upon them all. 34 there was not a needy person among them, for as many as were owners of lands or houses sold them and brought the proceeds of what was sold 35 and laid it at the apostles' feet, and it was distributed to each as any had need."

ACTS 4:32-35

DAY 21

Here we are on the last day of your "Basic Christianity" journey. So what now?

Today - join the cause of Jesus Christ and bring the good news of His Kingdom to everyone you can. See people saved by Him and become disciples of Him.

The best way for you to do this is to get discipled yourself, so you can then disciple others. A follower of Jesus will always make other followers of Jesus. You can join a small group in your church, ask your pastor or leader what discipleship looks like in your church context, or ask a friend to disciple you. Whatever it is, know that it's our personal responsibility to become and create followers of Jesus. Read and spend time in the gospels (Matthew, Mark, Luke, and John) to see what Jesus is like. Out of a loving relationship with Jesus, follow His example.

"Then Jesus came to them and said, 'All authority in heaven and on earth has been given to me. Therefore go and make disciples of all nations, baptizing them in the name of the Father and of the Son and of the Holy Spirit, and teaching them to obey everything I have commanded you. And surely I am with you always, to the very end of the age.'"

MATTHEW 28:18-20

NOTES

NOTES

NOTES

NOTES

NOTES

NOTES

NOTES

NOTES

NOTES

NOTES

NOTES

NOTES

NOTES

NOTES

NOTES

NOTES

Manufactured by Amazon.ca
Bolton, ON

25076862R00031